Cursive Handwriting Workbook

With Positive Affirmations

Newbee Publication

© 2021 Newbee Publication

ALL RIGHTS RESERVED

This book may not be reproduced or transmitted in any form or by any means, electronic or mechanical, without written permission from the author.

I HAVE THE POWER TO CREATE CHANGE

How to use

- To get the full benefit of this workbook, use different colour pens to make it exciting and improve mindfulness.

- Don't worry about if you go outside the lines because Practice makes perfect.

- Do not forget to colour images given on the page to relax and refresh your brain.

- The perfect time is when you have energy, and you think you can focus.

- Please write us if you find any design and quote difficult or not up to the mark; we will try to edit & update it.

- Share your work and experience with us by writing on Amazon or email – newbeepublication@gmail.com

- For more activity books and ideas, visit –

www.newbeepublication.com

I believe in myself.

I believe in myself

I believe in myself

I believe in myself

I believe in myself

I am Authentic to myself.

I am Authentic to myself

I am Authentic to myself

I am Authentic to myself

I am Authentic to myself

I am Authentic to myself

I am capable of achieving anything.
I am capable of achieving anything.
I am capable of achieving anything
I am capable of achieving anything
I am capable of achieving anything
I am capable of achieving anything

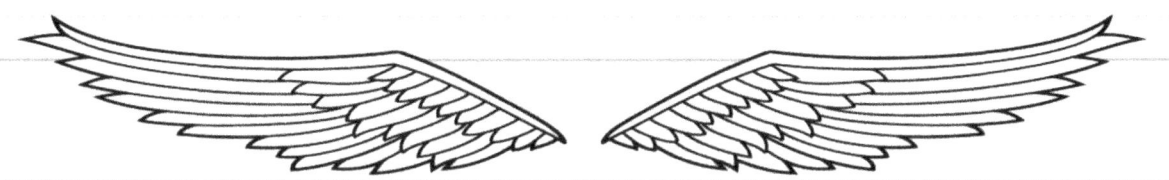

Every day my confidence goes strong.

Every day my confidence goes strong.

Every day my confidence goes strong

Every day my confidence goes strong

Every day my confidence goes strong

Every day my confidence goes strong

I know I can meet any challenge.

I know I can meet any challenge

I know I can meet any challenge

I know I can meet any challenge

I know I can meet any challenge

I know I can meet any challenge

I speak up my mind without hesitation.

I speak up my mind without hesitation.

I speak up my mind without hesitation

I speak up my mind without hesitation

I speak up my mind without hesitation

I speak up my mind without hesitation

I have total faith in my abilities.

I have total faith in my abilities

I have total faith in my abilities

I have total faith in my abilities

I have total faith in my abilities

I have total faith in my abilities

I have total faith in my abilities

I am learning a new thing every minute.

I am learning a new thing every minute.

I am learning a new thing every minute.

I am learning a new thing every minute.

I am learning a new thing every minute.

I am learning a new thing every minute.

I am learning a new thing every minute.

  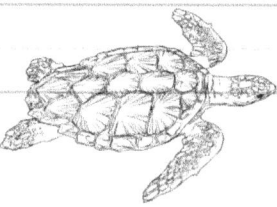  

I can always rely on my memory

I can always rely on my memory

I can always rely on my memory

I can always rely on my memory

I can always rely on my memory

I can always rely on my memory

I can always rely on my memory

I can tap into my memory easily

I can tap into my memory easily

I can tap into my memory easily

I can tap into my memory easily

I can tap into my memory easily

I can tap into my memory easily

I can tap into my memory easily

I remember things with accuracy and clarity.

I remember things with accuracy and clarity

I remember things with accuracy and clarity

I remember things with accuracy and clarity

I remember things with accuracy and clarity

I remember things with accuracy and clarity

I remember things with accuracy and clarity

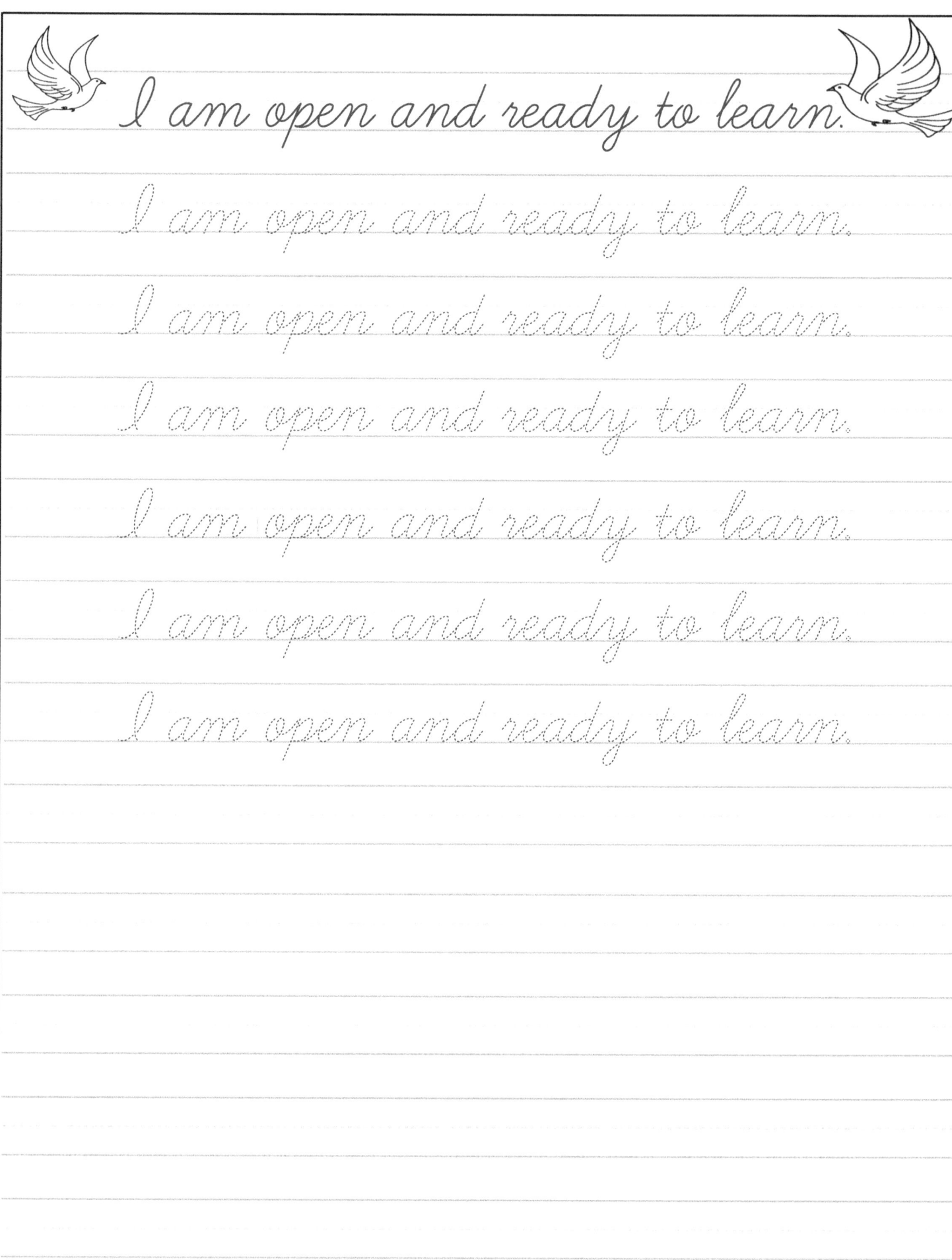

I am open and ready to learn.

I am open and ready to learn.
I am open and ready to learn.
I am open and ready to learn.
I am open and ready to learn.
I am open and ready to learn.
I am open and ready to learn.

I can be anything I want to be.

I can be anything I want to be.

I can be anything I want to be.

I can be anything I want to be.

I can be anything I want to be.

I can be anything I want to be.

I can be anything I want to be.

I stand up for what I believe in.

I stand up for what I believe in.

I stand up for what I believe in.

I stand up for what I believe in.

I stand up for what I believe in.

I stand up for what I believe in.

I stand up for what I believe in.

I am creative and calm.

I am creative and calm.

I am creative and calm.

I am creative and calm.

I am creative and calm.

I am creative and calm.

I am creative and calm.

I choose to think positive.

I choose to think positive.

I choose to think positive.

I choose to think positive.

I choose to think positive.

I choose to think positive.

I choose to think positive.

My ability to remember is amazing.

My ability to remember is amazing

My ability to remember is amazing

My ability to remember is amazing

My ability to remember is amazing

My ability to remember is amazing

My ability to remember is amazing

I will not put limits on my ability.

I will not put limits on my ability.

I will not put limits on my ability.

I will not put limits on my ability.

I will not put limits on my ability.

I will not put limits on my ability.

I will not put limits on my ability.

Remembering things is easy for me.

Remembering things is easy for me

Remembering things is easy for me

Remembering things is easy for me

Remembering things is easy for me

Remembering things is easy for me

Remembering things is easy for me

My memory is sharp and reliable.

My memory is sharp and reliable

My memory is sharp and reliable

My memory is sharp and reliable

My memory is sharp and reliable

My memory is sharp and reliable

My memory is sharp and reliable

I am surround myself with good people

I am surround myself with good people

I am surround myself with good people

I am surround myself with good people

I am surround myself with good people

I am surround myself with good people

I am surround myself with good people

I go after what I want And can do it

I go after what I want And can do it

I go after what I want And can do it

I go after what I want And can do it

I go after what I want And can do it

I go after what I want And can do it

I go after what I want And can do it

People admire my unwavering self-belief

People admire my unwavering self-belief

People admire my unwavering self-belief

People admire my unwavering self-belief

People admire my unwavering self-belief

People admire my unwavering self-belief

People admire my unwavering self-belief

I speak up my mind without hesitation

I speak up my mind without hesitation

I speak up my mind without hesitation

I speak up my mind without hesitation

I speak up my mind without hesitation

I speak up my mind without hesitation

I speak up my mind without hesitation

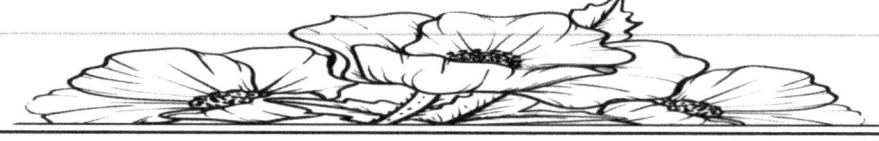

I am perfect just the way I am.

I am perfect just the way I am.

I am perfect just the way I am.

I am perfect just the way I am.

I am perfect just the way I am.

I am perfect just the way I am.

I am perfect just the way I am.

I stay cheerful and calm

I stay cheerful and calm

I stay cheerful and calm

I stay cheerful and calm

I stay cheerful and calm

I stay cheerful and calm

I stay cheerful and calm

I can control my own happiness

I can control my own happiness

I can control my own happiness

I can control my own happiness

I can control my own happiness

I can control my own happiness

I can control my own happiness

I get better every single day.

I get better every single day

I get better every single day

I get better every single day

I get better every single day

I get better every single day

I believe in my dreams.

I believe in my dreams.

I believe in my dreams.

I believe in my dreams.

I believe in my dreams.

I believe in my dreams.

It's okay to make mistakes.

It's okay to make mistakes.

It's okay to make mistakes.

It's okay to make mistakes.

It's okay to make mistakes.

It's okay to make mistakes.

I decide my own attitude.

I decide my own attitude.

I decide my own attitude.

I decide my own attitude.

I decide my own attitude.

I decide my own attitude.

My words have power.

My words have power.

My words have power.

My words have power.

My words have power.

My words have power.

My words have power.

My opinions matter.

My opinions matter.

My opinions matter.

My opinions matter.

My opinions matter.

My opinions matter.

My opinions matter.

My mistakes help me learn and grow.

My mistakes help me learn and grow.

My mistakes help me learn and grow.

My mistakes help me learn and grow.

My mistakes help me learn and grow.

My mistakes help me learn and grow.

I am free to make my own choices.

I am free to make my own choices.

I am free to make my own choices.

I am free to make my own choices.

I am free to make my own choices.

I am free to make my own choices.

I am free to make my own choices.

Good things are going to come to me.

Good things are going to come to me.

Good things are going to come to me.

Good things are going to come to me.

Good things are going to come to me.

I have control over my negative thoughts.

I have control over my negative thoughts.

I have control over my negative thoughts.

I have control over my negative thoughts.

I have control over my negative thoughts.

I have control over my negative thoughts.

I have control over my negative thoughts.

Being true to myself is what matters.

Being true to myself is what matters.

Being true to myself is what matters.

Being true to myself is what matters.

Being true to myself is what matters.

Being true to myself is what matters.

I am a good listener and a wonderful friend.

I am a good listener and a wonderful friend.

I am a good listener and a wonderful friend.

I am a good listener and a wonderful friend.

I am a good listener and a wonderful friend.

I am a good listener and a wonderful friend.

I am allowed to feel proud of myself.

I am allowed to feel proud of myself.

I am allowed to feel proud of myself.

I am allowed to feel proud of myself.

I am allowed to feel proud of myself.

I am allowed to feel proud of myself.

I don't need to be perfect to be accepted.

I don't need to be perfect to be accepted.

I don't need to be perfect to be accepted.

I don't need to be perfect to be accepted.

I don't need to be perfect to be accepted.

I don't need to be perfect to be accepted.

I speak to myself with kindness.

I speak to myself with kindness.

I speak to myself with kindness.

I speak to myself with kindness.

I speak to myself with kindness.

I speak to myself with kindness.

I speak to myself with kindness.

I consider other people's feelings.

I consider other people's feelings.

I consider other people's feelings.

I consider other people's feelings.

I consider other people's feelings.

I consider other people's feelings.

I am grateful to my body.

I am grateful to my body.

I am grateful to my body.

I am grateful to my body.

I am grateful to my body.

I am grateful to my body.

I am grateful to my body.

My body is strong and healthy.

My body is strong and healthy.

My body is strong and healthy.

My body is strong and healthy.

My body is strong and healthy.

My body is strong and healthy.

My body is strong and healthy.

I don't compare myself to others.

I don't compare myself to others.

I don't compare myself to others.

I don't compare myself to others.

I don't compare myself to others.

I don't compare myself to others.

I am an important part of my family.

I deserve to be accepted for my true self.

I deserve to be accepted for my true self.

I deserve to be accepted for my true self.

I deserve to be accepted for my true self.

I deserve to be accepted for my true self.

I deserve to be accepted for my true self.

I deserve to be accepted for my true self.

I calm my mind with my breath.

I calm my mind with my breath

I calm my mind with my breath

I calm my mind with my breath

I calm my mind with my breath

I calm my mind with my breath

I calm my mind with my breath

I peacefully resolve conflicts.

I peacefully resolve conflicts.

I peacefully resolve conflicts.

I peacefully resolve conflicts.

I peacefully resolve conflicts.

I peacefully resolve conflicts.

I peacefully resolve conflicts.

I am open to new ideas.

I am open to new ideas.

I am open to new ideas.

I am open to new ideas.

I am open to new ideas.

I am open to new ideas.

I deal with anger in healthy ways.

I deal with anger in healthy ways.

I deal with anger in healthy ways.

I deal with anger in healthy ways.

I deal with anger in healthy ways.

I deal with anger in healthy ways.

I deal with anger in healthy ways.

I find solutions to my problems.

I find solutions to my problems.

I find solutions to my problems.

I find solutions to my problems.

I find solutions to my problems.

I find solutions to my problems.

I find solutions to my problems.

I follow my dreams no matter what.

I follow my dreams no matter what

I follow my dreams no matter what

I follow my dreams no matter what

I follow my dreams no matter what

I follow my dreams no matter what

I follow my dreams no matter what

I get better every day in every way.

I get better every day in every way.

I get better every day in every way.

I get better every day in every way.

I get better every day in every way.

I get better every day in every way.

I get better every day in every way.

I am responsible for the words I speak.

I am responsible for the words I speak

I am responsible for the words I speak

I am responsible for the words I speak

I am responsible for the words I speak

I am responsible for the words I speak

I like creating new things and ask new questions.

I like creating new things and ask new questions

I accept help from others to achieve my goals.

I accept help from others to achieve my goals.

I accept help from others to achieve my goals.

I respect others even when
I don't agree with them.

I respect others even when
I don't agree with them.

I respect others even when
I don't agree with them.

I have the courage to share my true feelings and opinions.

I have the courage to share my true feelings and opinions.

I have the courage to share my true feelings and opinions.

I listen when others share their feelings and opinions.

I listen when others share their feelings and opinions.

I listen when others share their feelings and opinions.

I can handle any changes that come my way.

I can handle any changes that come my way.

I can handle any changes that come my way.

We all have something unique to contribute.

We all have something unique to contribute.

We all have something unique to contribute.

Everything works out for the best possible good.

Everything works out for the best possible good.

Everything works out for the best possible good.

I control my emotions;
    they don't control me.

I control my emotions;
    they don't control me.

I control my emotions;
    they don't control me.

I fill my day with hope and
face it with joy.

I fill my day with hope and
face it with joy.

I fill my day with hope and
face it with joy.

I can overcome anything that stands in my way.

I can overcome anything that stands in my way.

I can overcome anything that stands in my way.

I can overcome anything that stands in my way.

I am thankful that I can choose to learn even under challenging circumstances.

I am grateful for the family, friends and mentors that do believe in me.

I am thankful that I have so many choices, and I will use them wisely.

The more grateful I am, the more beauty I see.

Mary Davis

I am grateful that God is always in control.

I am grateful that God is always in control.

I am grateful that God is always in control.

I am grateful to my family and friends.

I am grateful for everything in my life.

I am grateful for everything in my life.

I am grateful for everything in my life.

I am so happy and grateful for my life.

I am so happy and grateful for my life.

I am so happy and grateful for my life.

I am getting better and better in all my ways.

I am getting better and better in all my ways

I am getting better and better in all my ways

I am so thankful that the universe is working for

my greater good.

www.ingramcontent.com/pod-product-compliance
Lightning Source LLC
Chambersburg PA
CBHW081337080526
44588CB00017B/2652